Human Body

By Kathleen Weidner Zoehfeld

SCHOLASTIC INC.

New York   Toronto   London   Sydney

Auckland   Mexico City   New Delhi   Hong Kong

Photo Credits

Cover: Junial/Istockphoto, London_England/Istockphoto, Odv/ Istockphoto; p. 3: Purestock/Getty-images; p. 4: Pappamaart/Istockphoto; p. 5: Nicolesy/Istockphoto; p. 6: Comstock/Gettyimages; p. 7: Pauline St Denis/Gettyimages; p. 8: Custom Medical Stock Photos; p. 9: Iconica/Gettyimages; p. 10: Photosindia/Gettyimages; p. 10 inset: Tom McCarthy/PhotoEdit; p. 11: Asla Images/Gettyimages; p.12: Dbuffoon/Istockphoto; p. 13: Fertnig/Istockphoto; p. 14: Ojo Images/ Gettyimages; p.15: Johnner Images/Gettyimages; p. 16: Custom Medical Stock Photos; p. 17: Nucleus Medical Art, Inc/ PhototakeUSA; p. 18: Blend Images/ Gettyimages; pp. 20-21: Digital Vision/ Gettyimages; p. 22: Richard Hutchings/PhotoEdit; p. 23: Brian Evans/ Photo Researchers; p. 25: Custom Medical Stock Photos; p. 26: Dk Stock/David Deas/ Gettyimages; p. 27: Nucleus Medical Art/Gettyimages; p. 28: Asla Images/ Gettyimages; p. 29: Taxi/Gettyimages; pp. 30-31: Iconica/ Gettyimages.

ISBN 978-0-545-23752-9

10 9 8 7 6 5 4 3 2 1   10 11 12 13 14/0

Printed in the U.S.A.   40
This edition first printing, September 2010

Your body has many parts.

eye

ear

hand

arm

chest

leg

foot

It has outside parts.

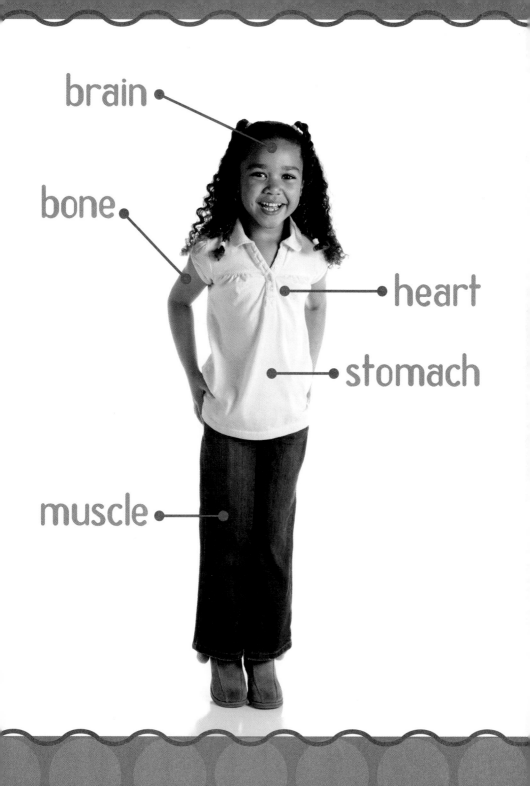

brain

bone

heart

stomach

muscle

And it has inside parts.

Most of your body is covered by skin. Your skin helps you feel if something is cold or hot, soft or hard, smooth or rough.

It also protects the inside of
your body.

Underneath your skin, you have bones. Bones protect important parts of your body like your brain and heart.

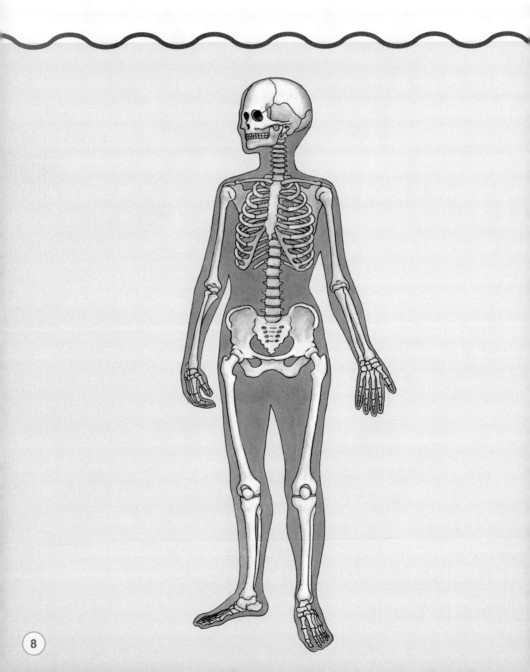

Different parts of your body send messages to your brain. Your brain helps you understand them all.

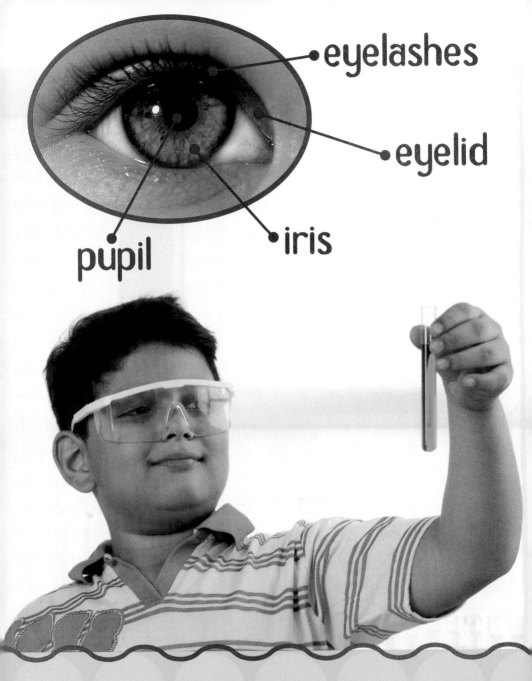

eyelashes

eyelid

iris

pupil

Your eyes send messages to your brain. Your brain tells you the shapes and colors of the things you see.

Your ears send messages to your brain. Your brain helps you understand all the sounds you hear.

The **taste buds** on your tongue send messages to your brain about the food you eat.

bitter

sour

sour

salty

salty

sweet

Your brain tells you if your food is salty, sour, bitter, or sweet.

Your nose sends messages to your brain. Your brain can tell if something smells good or bad.

When you touch a kitten, a message goes from your skin to your brain. Your brain tells you the kitten is soft.

Your brain sends messages to your muscles that tell them how to move. Muscles and bones help you run, walk, lift, and bend.

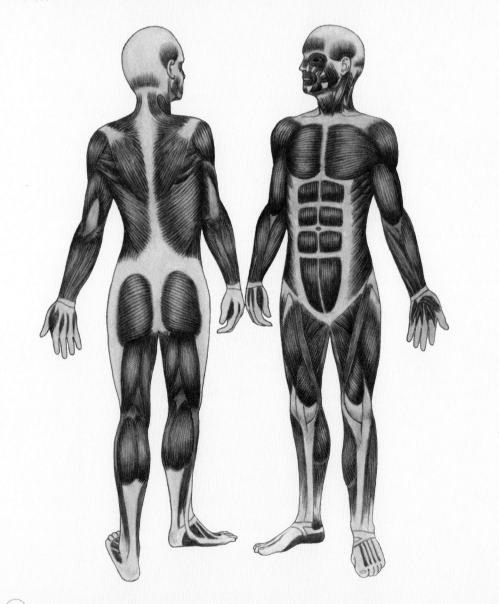

For all that muscle power, you need a lot of **energy**. And the best way to get energy is to eat!

When you swallow a bite of food, it moves down into your stomach.

Special juices in your stomach **digest** the food.

Then your body can take in simple things such as **sugars** from the food. Sugars give you energy.

To use the energy from the food you eat, your body needs **oxygen**.

When you breathe, your lungs take in oxygen from the air.

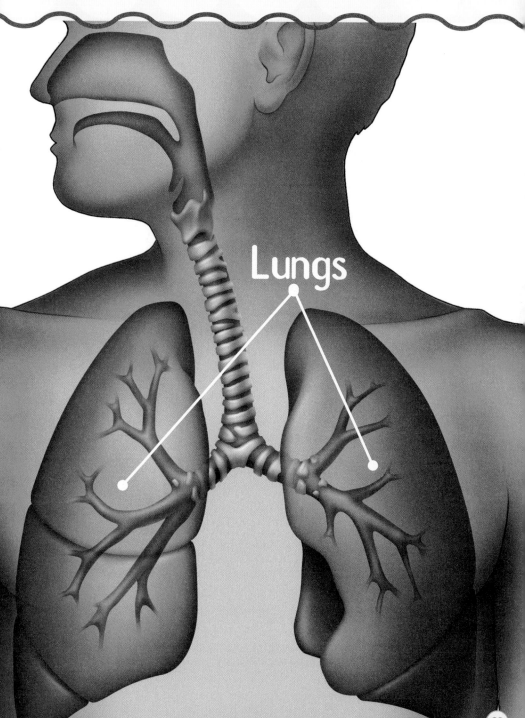

Lungs

The oxygen goes into your blood. Sugars from your food go into your blood, too.

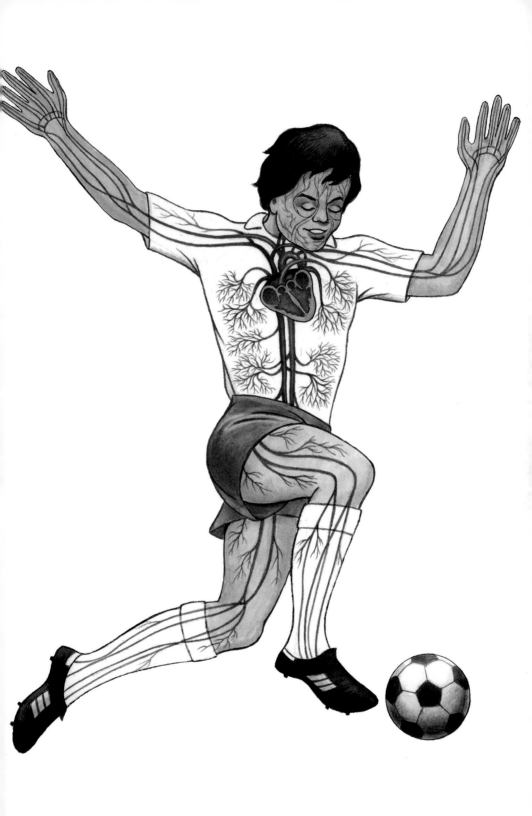

Your heart pumps blood full of oxygen and sugars from your food to all the parts of your body.

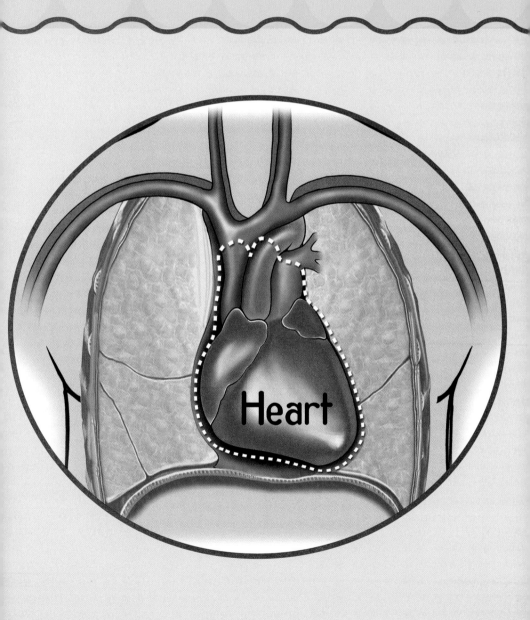

Heart

Even when you are asleep, your heart keeps pumping.

It is important to sleep and eat so your body can grow.

Although your body has many parts, they all work together to keep you alive.

Glossary

Digest – to break food down into simpler parts that can be taken in and used by the body for energy and for growing

Energy – the ability or power to do work

Oxygen (**ock**-suh-juhn)—one of the main gases in the air

Sugars – a simple, sweet part of most foods. Sugars can give energy to the body.

Taste buds – tiny, round bunches of cells found on the top of the tongue that help us taste our food